Where Is
GOD
When I'm
Afraid?

Where Is
GOD
When I'm Afraid?

Live with Confidence That He Is
Always with You

Pamela L. McQuade

VALUEBOOKS
An Imprint of Barbour Publishing, Inc.

Print ISBN 978-1-62416-997-7

eBook Editions:
Adobe Digital Edition (.epub) 978-1-63058-111-4
Kindle and MobiPocket Edition (.prc) 978-1-63058-112-1

Published by Value Books, an imprint of Barbour Publishing, Inc., P.O. Box 719, Uhrichsville, Ohio 44683, www.barbourbooks.com

Our mission is to publish and distribute inspirational products offering exceptional value and biblical encouragement to the masses.

Member of the
Evangelical Christian
Publishers Association

Printed in the United States of America.

CONTENTS

1. Where Is God When I'm Afraid? 7

2. Where Is God When I'm Afraid
   of Him? 25

3. Where Is God When People Disappoint
   and Hurt Me? 39

4. Where Is God When I Fear for My
   Family? 55

5. Where Is God When I'm Afraid
   to Fail? 67

6. Where Is God When Money Stresses
   Me Out? 81

7. Where Is God When the Future Looks
   Dim? 99

8. Where Is God When the World Seems
   Crazy? 115

9. Where Is God When My Health Is
   Failing? 131

10. Where Is God? He Is Always with
    You 147

1
WHERE IS GOD WHEN I'M AFRAID?

Every day, fears of all sorts knock at our doors, trying to make us believe imminent danger is about to enter our lives. Newspapers keep those anxieties before our eyes, and online news tracks it for us through the day—our smart phones and computers constantly remind us of the need to worry about local troubles and those across the world. TV newscasters describe disasters that could impact our personal lives, the threats to our livelihoods and families, and fears that some monster half a world away could destroy our country. The media delights in keeping us on edge and seems to attract plenty of people who enjoy living in a constant state of angst.

It's amazing how many problems exist in the world, and every day we may feel as if we have to worry about every one of them. We buy into our right to agonize over all of these disasters, personal and distant. Soon we begin to act as if there isn't peace in the Middle East because of something we did, though we have nothing to do with the political policies that fuel the fires there and know the biblical prophesies about the state of Israel and the end times. Anxiety rules our lives.

Anxiety rules our lives.

When we fall into personal fears, it's as if an internal fear salesman charmed his way in our front door and used a smooth line of insecurity marketing techniques starting with words like: "You'll never. . . ," "This awful thing will. . . ," or "Other people think. . . ." There's not a bit of good news in his sales pitch, but all too often we've acted as if it were the best news around and we couldn't wait to bring this thought pattern into our homes. Yet once we buy into anxieties, our minds run in circles and we can't ponder anything but some personal or global disaster. Like mice in a maze, we've readily become trapped in doubt and misery. And there seems to be no way out.

Besetting Fears

What fear really plucks your own last nerve? Is it the thought of losing all your money? Your relationships? Your spiritual stature in the church? Maybe it's a fear that comes when you look at the future and see political dangers ahead. Or perhaps fear of fear itself stops you in your tracks. Many apprehensions flit through our lives. But we all seem to have a few that rack our nerves more than others. A person who can ignore fears about where the world is headed in ten years may be trapped by fears for family. One who is confident about family may agonize over personal failures. All of us seem to have a special sensitivity to something. And of course, nothing keeps us from having more than one fear that frequently tugs at our hearts.

Whatever our besetting fears, we may dread even thinking about them. Whenever we can, we stuff them under the rug and ignore them until they become a stumbling block we constantly trip over. Or if we wake at night, we may worry over them the way a dog worries over a favorite bone.

Anxieties touch all our lives. None of us escape their clutches, though some of us may fear more often than others. But neither does fear have to control our lives. Though worries may pass through our minds, they don't have to take up residence.

AN ANATOMY OF FEAR

Couldn't God have stopped fear in its tracks? we may ask ourselves. *Why are we caught in this mess? Doesn't He give us promises about fear? And if so, why isn't He keeping them?*

Why did God allow fear to be part of our lives? In truth, life can be dangerous. God gave us a sense of fear to keep us from rushing into trouble without a second thought. Fear is the yellow bulb in God's traffic light, warning us that we should go a little slower. When we fear something, it's time to ease up and consider where we are going. Then we can reorganize our lives in a better way.

Fear is the yellow bulb in God's traffic light.

After the Fall, Satan and our own fallen natures took that natural warning system to a new, negative level. Instead of simply acting as a warning signal, fear began misdirecting our lives into a system that feeds on our own mistrust of God and the future we cannot see.

OUR OWN PART IN FEAR

Fear's trap is often at least partly of our own making. Satan and his minions are not entirely responsible. Why should they micromanage our affairs when all they need to do is give a touch here and there? A difficult situation comes up, and the minions of evil implant doubt that God will help. Then they allow our fertile imaginations to take over. Fueled by doubt, our own thoughts quickly come up with enough fears to fill our minds to overflowing—the enemy barely has to do a thing before we have fallen into his trap and he's heard the satisfying click of its door closing. With a tweak here and there, the evil one has us just where he wants us. Blinded by our own unbelief, we start asking where God is in this awful situation. Soon enough, we're blaming Him for our problems, and the evil one has us just where he wanted us all along. Caught in agitation, we'll lay the blame anywhere but at our own doors.

As we lie in the trap, our minds running at a thousand miles an hour, we ignore the simplest truth that most of our fears never materialize. How often have we been terrified that we'd lose our jobs, have a car accident, or lose a child or spouse? Sometimes we've worried our situations into truth, but more often, they've been the fruitless concerns of a trapped brain. Instead, perhaps we should ask ourselves, *How many of those fears have failed to come true?* And even if something did happen, what was the ultimate outcome? Maybe you lost your job and struggled for a while, only to find the best job you'd ever had. That long-term result was ultimately worth the times of real fear. And as a huge bonus, you learned to trust God during those days of trial. When we're facing troubles, it's hard to see it this way, but God often brings good out of real evil.

A certain amount of fear is normal in a bad situation. Paul, the brave apostle, admits a time of fear when everything seemed to be going wrong: "For,

God often brings good out of real evil.

when we were come into Macedonia, our flesh had no rest, but we were troubled on every side; without were fightings, within were fears" (2 Corinthians 7:5 KJV). The situation in Macedonia wasn't good, and Paul knew it. But he didn't let what was going on here on earth sabotage his work for God. Along with the fear, he recognized God's hand in the comfort that followed: "Nevertheless," he testifies in the next verse, "God, that comforteth those that are cast down, comforted us by the coming of Titus." God doesn't leave us in a desperate situation with no help. And Paul went on with the ministry that was given to him, trusting that the Lord who gave it to him would see him through.

WHEN FEAR STRIKES

But how do we deal with fear, when it attacks us and threatens to take us captive?

One of the worst things we can do is to give in to worry. Corrie ten Boom, who accomplished the dangerous task of hiding Jews in occupied Holland during World War II, warned: "Worry does not empty tomorrow of its sorrow, it empties today of its strength. It does not enable us to escape evil. It makes us unfit to face evil when it comes. It is the interest you pay on trouble before it comes." Wallowing in fear cannot help us take action against it; instead we will bypass opportunities and perhaps even see damage done to our spiritual lives.

We can begin by remembering that worry and fears are not gifts from God, who has "not given us a spirit of fear, but of power and of love and of a sound mind" (2 Timothy 1:7 NKJV). Anyone who has been wrapped in fear can testify that it does not lead to love and a sound mind. Instead, taking our fears out on others or constantly complaining could become our pattern of response, and that's not the way God wants us to live.

"Fear is faithlessness," George Macdonald explained, and he is right. When we focus on the what-ifs of life and agonize about them, we bring to pass our own downfall. As C. S. Lewis commented: "One is given strength to bear what happens to one, but not the one hundred and one different things that might happen." God cannot give us strength to endure things that will never happen.

Agonizing never provides a solution to our problems or gives us new plans that will help us avoid them. Nor will becoming a worrywart turn us to the greatest solution: entering into deeper communion with God. Instead, the more we worry, the more we find ourselves focusing on this world and its dangers and ignoring the One who has command of them all. Putting our eyes on the world denies God's power in it and His ability to save us from anything within creation. Essentially, as we worry, we give greater power to our Lord's enemies than we allow Him to have in our lives.

Agonizing never provides a solution to our problems

The way to sidetrack fear and its destruction in our lives is to draw nearer to our Lord, trusting that even the terrible emotions that interfere with our thoughts and rack our beings are not beyond His aid. As we seek His truths, our hearts and minds get off the track of fear and can focus on His strength and direction for our lives.

Why should we fear anything on this earth? There is One who is greater than them all, who sent

His Son to draw us near to Himself and die for all the sins that draw us in the opposite direction. This God who loves us so deeply also told us: "Be anxious for nothing, but in everything by prayer and supplication with thanksgiving let your requests be made known to [Me]" (Philippians 4:6 NASB). He is all-powerful and in control of everything. On the day He returns to earth, "People will faint from terror, apprehensive of what is coming on the world, for the heavenly bodies will be shaken" (Luke 21:26 NIV). But though we read these truths in scripture and give an accepting nod to their accuracy, we may still have a hard time putting their reality into our lives.

WHEN FEAR'S A SPECIAL AGONY

For some people, fear issues may be more than a simple lack of faith or worry over a situation. Some who believe in Jesus and have trusted their lives to Him still suffer from panic attacks. Not just a momentary fear or something that happens when a difficult situation is on their minds, these chronic experiences of debilitating fear may strike at any time, sometimes even in the middle of the night. For 2.4 million people in the United States, panic-attack symptoms, which may include a racing heart and chest pains, can make them worry they are experiencing a heart attack or fear they are dying. Their symptoms are more than a passing distrust of God. Real panic attacks affect sufferers' bodies and souls.

Those who experience panic attacks need to seek the best medical and Christian counseling care available. But even the most skilled doctors can't fully explain why panic attacks happen or what causes them, and developing a strong spiritual life may be a critical weapon in the arsenal that fights them. As with so many physical ailments, our spirits can be part of the solution.

Fighting Back

No matter how fear comes into our lives, we cannot respond to it by rolling over and playing dead. Instead, we need to recognize where it comes from and respond to this spiritual challenge.

Remember, "God has not given us a spirit of fear, but of power and of love and of a sound mind" (2 Timothy 1:7 NKJV). Not only has our Lord not given us fear, but also through Him we have the power to fight back against overwhelming doubts. His love, working in our lives, makes us whole and gives us a sound mental base from which we can view the world.

Fear need not command us. No knee-jerk emotional reaction should control our lives.

The truth is that whatever we feed in our spiritual lives can overtake us. When we feed the agonies of fear, we risk becoming sidelined from our spiritual lives and easily end up with seriously isolated lives that barely interact with those who can help us in the battle against it. We may run into church on Sunday morning and dash out at the end of the service because we fear that someone will ask how we're doing. Faced with the possibility of lying or having to tell the truth, we'd rather avoid both options. As we run away, our spiritual lives become even more limited.

No knee-jerk emotional reaction should control our lives.

But those who take a stand against fear, grab onto all the spiritual help available, and trust in God can have a completely different outcome. Instead of worrying, they can cast off fear and regain the peace of God: "Thou wilt keep him in perfect peace, whose mind is stayed on thee: because he trusteth in thee" (Isaiah 26:3 KJV).

Overcoming fear requires us to grab onto the

One who is never fearful, and as we cling to Him and follow His wise advice, we can begin to find our way out of the miasma of fear that clings to our souls and beings.

Challenging fear brings us face-to-face with a word we don't necessarily like: obedience. It's not a popular word in today's individualistic society. But loving God means obeying Him, and following His Word will trap the enemies of doubt and fear. "If we want the Word of God to have authority in our life," Tom Marshall comments, "there is only one way— obey it. If we want the Holy Spirit to have authority in our life, there is only one way—Obey Him. If we always obey impulses of fear or doubt or resentment, what will have authority over our minds? Fear, and doubt and resentment."

What will have authority over our minds?

And when we fear God, as the scripture commands, and seek to do His will, Oswald Chambers points out that "the remarkable thing about fearing God is that when you fear God you fear nothing else, whereas if you do not fear God you fear everything else."

STANDING UP AGAINST FEAR

One way to take a stand against fear is to make our devotion to God a serious part of our lives. That means reading scripture on a regular basis, so we can hear God's voice. When we read scripture daily and read enough of it that our conversation with Him is more than a sentence (or maybe a paragraph), we quickly find that the Word of God shows us the way. As we read a verse, it may suddenly jump off the page, providing hope, encouragement, or instruction. And the more we read His Word, the better we understand it and the One who gave it to us.

But standing up against fear means making God more than the focus of our lives for just a few minutes a day. Nicholas Herman, a seventeenth-century lay brother in a Carmelite monastery in Paris, France, provided useful advice on this. While working in the kitchen or acting as the monastery's cobbler, Nicholas sought to focus entirely on God. No matter what he did, his thoughts inclined toward the Savior. And he discovered "that in order to form a habit of conversing with God continually, and referring all we do to Him; we must at first apply to Him with some diligence: but that after a little care we should find His love inwardly excite us to it without any difficulty." The small book *Practice of the Presence of God*, a volume of conversations with and letters by Nicholas, has become a classic. Though he had no education to speak of, following his conversion at age eighteen, Nicholas had deeply studied the truths of God. His perceptions concerning the need for God to be the center of our lives have helped many live more faithfully for Him.

Though we cannot spend our days in a monastery, as we work in regular jobs, we can think of how God would have us act, do our jobs, and treat others. As we walk from place to place or move from one task to another, we can lift up a quick prayer or ponder the greatness of our Lord. And the more we continually make God the center of our lives, the less room fear will have within us.

The more we continually make God the center of our lives, the less room fear will have within us.

When fear begins to attack, we can determinedly give our doubts up to God and change our thinking. By focusing on scripture and prayer, we give our thoughts another direction. As we think of ways we can help others, we turn doubts into actions for our Lord.

When God has His proper place in our lives, what fear can stand before Him?

When we put trust in God, how does that affect how we handle fear?

_____

_____

_____

_____

_____

_____

_____

_____

_____

_____

What are some day-to-day fears you have that you can lift up to God right now?

_____

_____

_____

_____

_____

_____

_____

_____

_____

_____

What other spiritual tools can we use to reduce the grasp that fear has on our lives?

2
WHERE IS GOD
WHEN I'M AFRAID OF HIM?

If God loves us so much and wants us to turn to Him for help, the solution to a fear problem should be easy, shouldn't it? We pray a simple prayer for help, and it's all done.

In a perfect world, no doubt it would work that way. We'd read the scriptures that tell of Jesus' love and command us to seek His help, and we'd do so. When fear attacked again, we'd grab onto our Savior's hand and let Him lead us through our spiritual pains.

But more often than not, fear sweeps over us when we aren't even looking. Before we know it, we're caught up in our own brand of angst, and by then even the thought of calling on Jesus has become painful. *Will God even hear me?* we wonder. *Does He care?*

Instead of trusting in the One who invites us to seek His aid, we find we're afraid to even ask. After all, isn't this the same God who judges our sins? And haven't we fallen far short of His requirements yet again? Aware that "it is a terrifying thing to fall into the hands of the living God," we find ourselves at a distance from the Savior who is most eager to help (Hebrews 10:31 NASB).

APPROACHING GOD
We may not think of it quite that clearly, and we may

not have that scripture in mind, but our spirits almost naturally seem to respond with doubts. The fact is, we often find it hard to approach God with our fears.

We often find it hard to approach God with our fears.

Some of how we respond depends upon our view of God, which is often based on our spiritual backgrounds. Ask yourself, *Who do I see God as?* When you look at God, who do you primarily see—Judge or Savior? Those who see Him as Judge over their lives are more likely to find it difficult to approach God when fear strikes.

But the prophet Isaiah promised God's people:

"But as for you, Israel my servant,
· Jacob my chosen one,
descended from Abraham my friend,
I have called you back from the ends of the earth,
saying, 'You are my servant.'
For I have chosen you
and will not throw you away.
Don't be afraid, for I am with you.
Don't be discouraged, for I am your God.
I will strengthen you and help you.

I will hold you up with my victorious right hand.
See, all your angry enemies lie there,
confused and humiliated.
Anyone who opposes you will die
and come to nothing.
You will look in vain
for those who tried to conquer you.
Those who attack you
will come to nothing."

ISAIAH 41:8–12 NLT

Fearful Christians might also focus on this passage that shows God's deep love for His people:

Whosoever shall confess that Jesus
is the Son of God, God dwelleth in him,
and he in God. And we have known
and believed the love that God hath to us.
God is love; and he that dwelleth in love dwelleth in
God, and God in him. Herein is our love made perfect,
that we may have boldness in the day of judgment:
because as he is, so are we in this world.
There is no fear in love; but perfect love
casteth out fear: because fear hath torment.
He that feareth is not made perfect in love.
We love him, because he first loved us.

1 JOHN 4:15–19 KJV

If we are in God because we've confessed our sins and trusted in Jesus, we need not fear His judgment. Jesus has taken it for us, and we are safe in Him.

But even those of us convinced that our Savior loves us deeply may have times when we hesitate to completely throw our lot in with God. When we need to approach Him, we may begin to ask ourselves which would be worse—to fall into His fearsome clutches or experience the dangers of worldly fears that are so familiar to us. Though we don't like our fears, at least we know what they require of us. If we place ourselves in God's hands, will we end up in a place we like even less, in a place that will require painful obedience to Him? Maybe He will expect us to take charge of our finances, instead of worrying about them. And that would mean we couldn't engage in our favorite pastimes. Or maybe we'd be required to forgive a fellow churchgoer whom we've disliked for many years. Though turning to God is certainly the best solution, it isn't always a rose-petal-strewn path either.

Though we don't like our fears, at least we know what they require of us.

Fearing and Loving God

Following Jesus isn't always easy, because much as we love Him, we also know, as C. S. Lewis said, that "he is not a tame lion." We cannot count on the fact that He will never make us face a challenge we'd prefer to avoid. That's because, much as Jesus loves us, He looks to the long-term benefit in our lives. If we will become spiritually stronger from experiencing a trial, He will not step in and take it all away. Unlike many earthly parents, who seek to help their children avoid any hardship, God is a hardy parent who allows some pain in our lives because He knows it will benefit us in the long run. Maybe that's why all of us still retain a little bit of fear of our heavenly Father.

But doesn't the Bible say we should fear Him?

Yes, the Bible frequently describes fear as an appropriate response to God's great power and judgment. For example, Isaiah 13:1–9 describes the day of the Lord and the terror it brings to Babylon. But the last verse says: "See, the day of the LORD is coming—a cruel day, with wrath and fierce anger—to make the land desolate and destroy the sinners within it" (NIV). God is attacking not His own people but those who have never accepted Him. These sinners never recognized His authority or turned to Him for help. Though He reached out to them, they denied Him and turned to other gods. So wrath was God's appropriate response.

But the fear that the Bible describes as it relates to those who love Him is completely different. God is asking those who have turned to Him in repentance not to run in terror from Him but to come to Him. The believer's fear of God, based in respect for Him, is positive and brings benefits: "In the fear of the LORD one has strong confidence, and his children will have a refuge. The fear of the LORD is a fountain of life, that one may turn away from the snares of death" (Proverbs 14:26–27 ESV). This emotion is a proper awe of our loving God that causes us to seek His will and obey Him: "To fear the LORD is to hate evil; I hate pride and arrogance, evil behavior and perverse speech" (Proverbs 8:13 NIV). A right fear of God sets the foundation for our whole lives, if we allow it to: "The fear of the LORD is the beginning of wisdom, and knowledge of the Holy One is understanding" (Proverbs 9:10 NIV).

The believer's fear of God, based in respect for Him, is positive.

So why aren't many believers experiencing this kind of wonderful knowledge of God? Perhaps it's because they do not understand His nature and the love He has for us. Lots of Christians relate well to Jesus, but speak of the Father, and they are more likely to be uncertain about His love. After all, they wonder, isn't God the Father the One who judges us and Jesus the One who saves us? How can you draw close to someone when you expect retribution at any minute?

To have that point of view is to have a false understanding of God. The Father and Jesus are not divided in personality or spirit. Jesus declared: "I and my Father are one" (John 10:30 KJV). Just so, anyone who loves the Son is loved by the Father, who sent Him to save us. There is no division between the love of the Father and Son for His people, as Jesus testified to repeatedly during His ministry:

He that hath my commandments, and keepeth them,
he it is that loveth me: and he that loveth me shall
be loved of my Father, and I will love him, and will
manifest myself to him.
JOHN 14:21 KJV

Jesus answered and said unto him, If a man love me,
he will keep my words: and my Father will love him,
and we will come unto him,
and make our abode with him.
JOHN 14:23 KJV

For the Father himself loveth you,
because ye have loved me,
and have believed that I came out from God.
JOHN 16:27 KJV

Behold, what manner of love the Father
hath bestowed upon us,
that we should be called the sons of God:
therefore the world knoweth us not,
because it knew him not.
1 JOHN 3:1 KJV

The love that saved the world was the Father's brainchild, the culmination of His desire to undo all the ills that came to us in the Fall of man. When we can grab hold of the reality of the Father's love for us, we become certain that we are truly loved and no longer fear His retribution.

Still, that powerful love doesn't mean our heavenly Father allows us to walk all over Him: "For whom the LORD loveth he correcteth; even as a father the son in whom he delighteth" (Proverbs 3:12 KJV). Fatherhood comes with a responsibility toward the child's development. That's why God will not always protect us from facing challenges here on earth.

Though God does not allow us to avoid all earthly strife, He promises something even better:

He will walk with us, no matter what we face. Nothing comes into our lives that doesn't also go through Him. Remember, God has made His abode in the Christian (John 14:23), so what we live through, He also experiences, through the Holy Spirit who abides in us.

Our Savior wants to help us though every trial.

Where is God when we are afraid of Him? Walking with us, turning our hearts to Himself, and loving us in every way that we will let Him. Let's not turn from our Savior, when He wants to welcome us into His open arms and help us through every trial. As Warren Wiersbe astutely notes: "It is good to remind ourselves that the will of God comes from the heart of God and that we need not be afraid."

Should we, as believers, fear God? How does fear of God affect our relationship with Him?

How does fear of retribution impact our decision to go to God with our fears?

3
WHERE IS GOD
WHEN PEOPLE DISAPPOINT
AND HURT ME?

Chances are good that if you've lived in this world for more than a day, someone has had the opportunity to offend or hurt you. That's because God is perfect, but people are not. And those who are closest to us, our family, dearest friends, and spiritual companions along the walk to heaven, are able to hurt us most because they touch the softest part of our hearts.

But disappointment doesn't stop there. We also hurt the ones we most love, because we reach the most delicate spots in their hearts. And often, when hearts are hurting, people say harsh words they'd never have spoken in a cooler, calmer moment. Those hurts can last many years, if we don't seek forgiveness. So we always need to remember to treat people as somewhat fragile cargo, since they all have hearts that can be easily broken.

TREATING OTHERS TENDERLY

No matter how little we relish the idea, God makes it clear that we are His representatives on earth, and with that role, we have the responsibility to be a good witness to the world for Him. That includes dealing kindly and lovingly with others.

The apostle Paul penned this description of the role we have between God and humanity:

For God was in Christ,
reconciling the world to himself,
no longer counting people's sins against them.
And he gave us this wonderful
message of reconciliation.
So we are Christ's ambassadors;
God is making his appeal through us.
We speak for Christ when we plead,
"Come back to God!"
For God made Christ, who never sinned,
to be the offering for our sin,
so that we could be made right
with God through Christ.
2 CORINTHIANS 5:19–21 NLT

Jesus also called us to relate to fellow believers in love: "So now I am giving you a new commandment: Love each other. Just as I have loved you, you should love each other. Your love for one another will prove to the world that you are my disciples" (John 13:34–35 NLT). How can we call people to God or love them when we unnecessarily offend them, speak harsh words to them, or treat them badly? They will hardly get the message our Lord has in mind to pass on. Instead they will see Him as a harsh or wicked master, one whom they want nothing to do with, or they will see us as hypocrites, bad examples of what it means to be a Christian. That's why all the things we do and say are so important to God. And it's as important to Him that we are on the receiving end of good words and behavior as it is that we give them to others.

Living consistently for God is one of the hardest things we do for Him. As we grow more deeply in God, we may improve our track record, but treating others lovingly is always going to be a challenge, since sin impacts every Christian, and we all tend to look out for ourselves better than we do one another.

Living consistently for God is one of the hardest things we do for Him.

God does not command us to take on anything He will not also empower us to do, so we know we are not left alone in this challenge. And as we grow in faith we find ourselves able to love more consistently because the Spirit works in our hearts and minds. "We don't need to write to you about the importance of loving each other," Paul told the Thessalonian church, "for God himself has taught you to love one another" (1 Thessalonians 4:9 NLT). As we study under the Savior, we become more faithful Christians; though we may not obey every command perfectly, our lives take on a new shape, and we have many more desires that reflect His love for us. Those attitudes shine through as our testimony to Him.

Perhaps that's why, as growing Christians, we can find it particularly hard when someone else disappoints us. Whether it's an unsaved family member or a fellow church member, our tender hearts can be easily torn when someone else doesn't recognize the need to treat us kindly. Softened by our faith, our hearts may be even more hurt than they would have been before we knew Jesus.

WHEN OTHERS HURT US

Pained hearts can cause people to attack each other like sharks. Emotions easily empower us in particularly nasty ways. But God's call to love one another does not end at the point where someone else does us wrong. Indeed, that may be the very time when God can do His best work in and through our lives. It does not matter who hurt us or why. God calls on us to live in forgiveness,

God calls on us to live in forgiveness, just as He forgave us.

just as He forgave us. "And be ye kind one to another, tenderhearted, forgiving one another, even as God for Christ's sake hath forgiven you" (Ephesians 4:32 KJV). It may take time and effort to reach the place where our hearts and minds can do that, but every day of our lives, we should grow in forgiveness, under God's grace.

Consider the wrongs done to Joseph by his brothers. Scripture makes it clear that young Joseph was far from perfect. A wiser man would have been careful about how he shared his dreams with his older brothers, who clearly would not appreciate being told he would rule over them. Joseph only spoke the truth as God had revealed it, but he did so rather thoughtlessly. How much better his life might have been if he'd considered how his words might hurt his siblings and even his parents.

Joseph's angry brothers were certainly out of God's will when they decided to get this young upstart out of their lives immediately and sold Joseph into slavery. Selfishly, they aimed to destroy their irritating brother's life forever. But despite the worst this family had to offer, God still worked in Joseph's life.

Many of us have had rough relationships with others. Maybe the harm has been even less deserved than it was in Joseph's case. But the story of Joseph and his hurtful brothers still helps us learn how to respond to the pains caused by people in our lives. After all, even if some of our experiences have been more painful, most of us have not been betrayed by nearly a dozen siblings at the same time.

After years of suffering as a slave and working hard for masters of a foreign nation, Joseph found himself second in command in Egypt. We're unlikely to find ourselves in Joseph's high position with the ability to end the lives of those who hurt us, but almost certainly we will come to a time when, like Egypt's second in command, we will have to make a decision: Will we forgive or hold a grudge forever?

Will we forgive or hold a grudge forever?

Maybe it was good that the brothers had been separated for years and had a different perspective on past sins. Joseph responded wisely, neither rushing into judgment of his brothers nor ignoring the ills of the past. Perhaps because God had prospered him in his new land, Joseph understood the importance of second chances. He decided to test his siblings and see if they had learned how wrong they had been to force slavery upon him. Would they repeat the offense, given the opportunity? So Joseph set up his full brother, Benjamin, to find out if their half brothers would betray the youngest child.

No question that Joseph remembered every word and action of the betrayal his half brothers had perpetrated against him. He could have let that fester through the years and turn him bitter. But it's unlikely a man with that attitude would have prospered in many things, as God had prospered Joseph (Genesis 39:2). Still, here was the chance to see into the hearts of the men who had done him wrong and perhaps to set the record straight. So Joseph had his servants plant a cup in Benjamin's sack of grain then accuse his youngest brother of theft.

When his half brothers stood up for Benjamin, a bitter Joseph might have wondered whether to rejoice or feel sorrow, but scripture shows no sign that Joseph really wanted the vengeance that could have been his. Instead he spoke tenderly to his siblings and showed that he had begun to understand God's purpose behind all the family turmoil: "God sent me ahead of you to preserve for you a remnant on earth and to save your lives by a great deliverance. So then, it was not you who sent me here, but God. He made me father to Pharaoh, lord of his entire household and ruler of all Egypt" (Genesis 45:7–8 NIV).

Joseph never told his brothers they were right to abuse him by selling him into slavery. That would have been untrue. Instead, he focused on the will of God. And where Egypt's second in command could not have condoned slavery from his brothers' hands, he could accept it from God as part of His larger plan. In the end, God prospered Joseph because He turned to Him in the dire situation. And through one man's terrible situation, God blessed all the people of Israel.

Through one man's terrible situation, God blessed all the people of Israel.

An interesting story in Genesis 50:15–21 indicates how long the brothers carried knowledge of their wrongdoing and guilt for it. When their father, Jacob, died, the brothers feared Joseph would finally take retribution on them and told him it was their father's wish that he might forgive them. Then they indicated their own remorse and offered to be his slaves. Joseph repeated what he'd told them already: God meant this for good. Then he offered to care for his siblings and their families. Joseph's forgiveness was wide and deep, just as ours needs to be.

Do we have awful situations in our lives? Have at least some of them been caused by those who love us? Yes.

Are those situations so difficult and impossible that God cannot rescue them? No. He is in control of the whole of creation. Is your loved one somehow outside creation, a being much larger than God? No. That means God is in control of anyone in this world who can do you harm. And He can rectify any harm that has been done to you, if only you follow Him and walk in His ways.

God's rescue may not come in a moment. Perhaps it will take many years, as in Joseph's case, but you can count on it that if you follow Him, good things will come of your obedience. You may see things set right on this earth, or it make take until you see all things judged in eternity, but

God's rescue may not come in a moment.

God will not forget your situation. "What is the price of two sparrows—one copper coin?" Jesus asked His disciples. Then He promised, "But not a single sparrow can fall to the ground without your Father knowing it. And the very hairs on your head are all numbered" (Matthew 10:29–30 NLT). If God can count our hairs, how much more does He know about every interaction we have with others? Nothing is beyond His knowledge.

When others disappoint us, God is not far away. If we have been faithful in studying His Word, we know He wants us to respond with love and forgiveness. But sometimes even the best Christians may give way to anger and speak words that do not reflect the love of Christ. As soon as possible, then, we need to confess our wrongdoing to Christ and the person we have offended.

If we keep short accounts of our wrongdoings and deal with them quickly, our lives will be much more peaceful and filled with the blessings of the Spirit. Long accounts of "he did this to me" or "she said that about me" will not glorify God or bless our lives.

Being a Christian is all about forgiveness—for us and for others. Each of us lives and moves in forgiveness because Jesus forgave our deepest sins and calls on us to follow His example. As hard as forgiveness is to offer, it's the way to peace with ourselves, each other, and our Lord.

When we fear God, we never need to fear another person (Psalm 118:6; Isaiah 51:7; Matthew 10:28). By placing ourselves in His hands alone, we have security in our futures and in our relationships. Though others may conspire against us or just say cruel things, God stands by us, encouraging and helping.

That does not mean God will smooth out all

our relationships in a moment. But we know He is working in our lives and those of others when we place ourselves in His hands. Then, with the psalmist, we can testify: "The LORD is with me; I will not be afraid. What can mere mortals do to me?" (Psalm 118:6 NIV).

"The Lord is with me; I will not be afraid" (PSALM 118:6 NIV).

How can our actions toward others affect how they feel about God?

When we live in forgiveness, how does that affect our relationships with others? Our relationship with God?

4
WHERE IS GOD
WHEN I FEAR FOR MY FAMILY?

Loving others deeply carries a risk with it. For the more we care, the more easily we hurt when things go wrong. Many people solve this problem by avoiding caring too deeply for others because they fear the pain that comes with loss. What a lonely way to live.

God recognized the need people have for others way back when Adam was in the Garden of Eden all alone, except for the animals. As wonderful as those animals were, they hadn't quite hit the spot in Adam's heart. So God made another human to keep the man company. He put Adam to sleep, removed a rib, and used it to fashion the woman he would love. Eve was designed not merely as a sexual partner. She's described as a "helper" (Genesis 2:23 NIV). In God's design, two people, man and woman, were meant to live together to aid each other—they were designed to be a God-made team that serves Him, others, and each other. When life became tough, this pair was meant to take things on together.

From that kind of established home came children, who were to learn firsthand, from their parents, what it means to love God and serve others. From there, the story was designed to continue for generation after generation.

In a perfect world, that would be a recipe for bliss. But again, humans, even the best of us, are not perfect. Instead of helping one another, we hurt our families, and our families hurt us, too. Sometimes we harm each other so badly that we think things can never be healed. But with God working in our lives, it is amazing what traumas we can recover from, what hurts can be forgiven, when we stop making excuses for ourselves and together commit to living our family lives the way He designed them to be.

With God working in our lives, it is amazing what hurts can be forgiven.

In order for things to work that way, we need to know what God has in mind for the family. As we study God's Word, we can garner plenty of practical advice on godly living, and much of what the Word says generally about living well with others applies perfectly to our families. Following this advice, we can become skilled at relationships in our homes and out.

But won't such tight relationships with our families only make our fears worse? Now that we have what we've always desired, won't the fear increase tenfold? Surely one of the greatest fears anyone feels is the fear of loss of life. *What would I do without my mate?* we may ask. And in an age when schools are suddenly and easily attacked, we may ask ourselves, *What if someone harmed my child?* Life in this world, we may tell ourselves, is cheap. The unthinkable could happen any moment. And we might be right, if we left God out of the equation.

Abraham was chosen by God—what more could a man ask for? The Creator declared that His people would be established through Abraham's line. Most of us might figure that would give a man some serious advantages in life. If God chose us, maybe we'd have a cushy life. Everything would run smoothly, because God would make everything easy. Our motto might be: "Every valley shall be raised up, every mountain and hill made low; the rough ground shall become level, the rugged places a plain" (Isaiah 40:4 NIV). The problem is that God never gave that promise to us for our daily lives. He never promised that Abraham would have a slick life that would slide him into heaven, and He doesn't promise it to us either.

If Abraham hadn't discovered that earlier, he would have known it on the day God called him to make a sacrifice. "Take your son, your only son, whom you love—Isaac—and go to the region of Moriah," God commanded. "Sacrifice him there as a burnt offering on a mountain I will show you" (Genesis 22:2 KJV). What greater sacrifice could God ask of His man? We may ask ourselves, *How could Abraham stand it?*

How could He ask this of him?

Abraham went to the mountain with everything for the sacrifice except the usual animal for the offering. When they arrived, Isaac asked about the sacrifice, and his father responded that God would provide one. Abraham knew his Lord and trusted in the promise that Isaac would begin a new line of people. Even if God were to require the sacrifice, Abraham reasoned, could He not bring his son back to life? (See Hebrews 11:19.) What amazing faith!

At the end of the story God intervened. That day a ram died in Isaac's place, and Abraham had made his commitment plain.

Often God asks us to put our relationships on His altar. We come to a fork in the road, and we need to choose. Will we be faithful to that special loved one or Him? In the end, if we gave up our faith for family, we would find ourselves miserable. Even the best worldly relationships cannot take the place of God in our lives. And frequently, once we pass that test and put Him first, God hands us back a new, improved human relationship. But even if He doesn't, we have drawn

> *Often God asks us to put our relationships on His altar.*

closer to Him and gained strength for the harder way He requires of us. Whatever happens, if we grab onto His hand and hold tight, we can pass through any storm that comes our way.

Yet it may not be the end of our story that's hard. It's getting through the troubles of the test. While we walk the difficult path through any storm, we may feel God has abandoned us. If we end up in an argument with a spouse or child, we may ask ourselves what happened and how God could allow such outbursts. Or when a loved one is seriously ill, we may feel ourselves stretched to the max and wonder why God hasn't miraculously intervened.

In that moment when we appear to be facing complete destruction of all we've known relationally, we cannot turn our backs on God. Instead we need to remember that God has been good to us in so many ways, and He will be good to us even in this. The One who cared enough to send His own Son to die for us may not spare us all the pain, but He will walk with us in it. If we turn to Him, casting all our cares on Him, sudden peace may fill our souls. We won't know the end yet, but having trusted in the One who holds it in His hands, we know He will not fail us. With deep troubles, God often sends profoundly satisfying comfort, if we throw our lives into His hands.

But what of hard times that are less dramatic,

the days when we feel ground down by continual bickering or confusion over the future?

Is God with us any less on the more ordinary days when that last nerve is plucked until we believe we can't bear it anymore? Has the very ordinariness of the situation made God impotent? If you've read your Bible, you know the answer: God is all-powerful, even over the ordinary, frustrating day. He's as much with us when a child is having trouble in school as He is when a life hangs in the balance.

God is all-powerful, even over the ordinary, frustrating day.

Yet, no matter what troubles we face, our feelings may still fight with us, dragging us away from faith. That's when we need to remember that faith is not feelings. Wonderful as they can be, feelings are not the be all and end all of our existence. They are often a result of the things we face every day—stresses and strains or delightful moments. But when we let feelings run the show, our cart pulls our horse. Often that spells disaster, since feelings come and go with whatever we experience. As a response to a situation, they are fine, but they should not run the show.

If we put our faith in God and trust Him with

every part of our relationships, we trust in someone much more secure than anything we feel. Our feelings may scream "disaster" at us, but if we are following our Lord, reading His Word to find out how we should act, and loving our families as He commands, we cannot face a complete disaster. Troubles may take us down a side rail for a time, but they will not wreck the train. In fact, in the end, we'll find the train just where it should be. But, as Abraham discovered, sometimes that train travels through deep tests to arrive at commitment.

A. W. Tozer recognized the temptation to grab our relationships back into our own hands when he said: "We are often hindered from giving up our treasures to the Lord out of fear for their safety; this is especially true when those treasures are loved relatives and friends. But we need have no such fears. Our Lord came not to destroy but to save. Everything is safe which we commit to Him, and nothing is really safe which is not so committed."

Feel safe in committing your loved ones to God's hands

Whether it's a minor matter or the most critical one you can imagine, feel safe in committing your loved ones to God's hands. He will never drop them.

If we put our faith in God and trust him with our relationships, how does that affect our lives?

What worldly relationships do we tend to put first, before God? How does that affect our relationship with Him?

5
WHERE IS GOD
WHEN I'M AFRAID TO FAIL?

Fear of failure may be a particularly difficult anxiety, since we know we all miss the mark in some ways. *Aren't we sinners, incapable of getting it all right? How can we do anything but fail?* we may ask ourselves as we struggle with this fear.

True, sin causes us to fail in many ways. Even when we try with all our might to do right, we have an accident on the way to work, slip up in a detail on the job, or have less-than-perfect home lives. With all that failure going on, it's a challenge to feel confident. But God never calls us to self-confidence; He calls us to obedience.

Feeling overwhelmed by failure, we need to remember the advice of Winston Churchill, the British prime minister who navigated his country through many dark days during World War II: "Success is not final, failure is not fatal: it is the courage to continue that counts." As long as we continue in our spiritual lives, God can draw us from failure into success. But as we look to add to our achievements, we need to be seeking the success He has in mind. Sometimes our problem with failure is not that we

"Success is not final, failure is not fatal: it is the courage to continue that counts."

have failed to reach our goal, but we have not reached the goal God has in mind for us. When we're constantly seeking to do His will, even if we don't achieve all our goals, we cannot fail, since spiritual success is never failure.

But even when we miss the mark spiritually, we are not the only believers who have ever fallen short. The Bible describes plenty of people who did something wrong—often something very large that affected the rest of their lives. But, if they repented, God neither condemned them on earth nor kicked them out of heaven. As our loving Savior, Jesus is not looking for an opportunity for harsh criticism. Instead, He's using every failure to draw us closer to Him.

CONTENT WITH FAILURE?

"My great concern," stated Abraham Lincoln, "is not whether you have failed, but whether you are content with your failure." There's a lot of wisdom in those words. Will we be content with failure or move beyond it?

One very sad biblical story appears in Numbers 13–14 when the twelve spies went into the promised land after God first brought His people to their new country. Ten came back with a report that said, "The land is wonderful, but the people there are too powerful. We should turn back." Two spies trusted that in God's power the Hebrew people could overcome.

How terribly disappointed the people who trusted in that majority opinion became. They rebelled against Moses, Aaron, and those two faithful spies, Caleb and Joshua. But their real rebellion was against God, not His messengers. As a result, God condemned the rebels to wander in the desert for the rest of their lives. Only the two faithful spies entered the promised land and then only after sharing those many years of wandering.

Scripture doesn't tell us how those ten men felt about what happened. Did they mentally kick themselves for the rest of their lives, or did they believe they'd been right all along? Certainly as Joshua and his people conquered the land, the unfaithful spies' descendants would have seen how wrong their forefathers had been.

When Joshua and Caleb objected to the majority opinion, these ten men had the opportunity to change their minds, but they didn't. Pigheadedly, they pushed the Hebrews down the road of bad decision making. If only they had recognized the truth in the minority opinion—that God would enable them to conquer a land that seemed much too dangerous—everyone could have avoided forty years of desert travel. Caleb and Joshua had reported, "The land we passed through and explored is exceedingly good. If the LORD is pleased with us, he will lead us into that land, a land flowing with milk and honey, and will give it to us" (Numbers 14:7–8 NIV). But without repentance and trust in God, the spies and all Israel were sent back to do forty years of laps in the desert. Their refusal to do things God's way gave them no recourse than to wallow in their own failure.

The greatest danger in failure is for us to start avoiding God with our failure.

But the spies are not the only people in the Bible who refused an opportunity to learn from mistakes and make life right again. Judas, who hanged himself in despair (Matthew 27:5), and Saul, who killed himself on the battlefield when the tide had turned against him (1 Samuel 31:4), are examples of failure in its worst and most deadly form.

The greatest danger in failure is for us to start avoiding God with our failure.

What We Do with Failure

The Bible also describes the lives of a number of people who failed miserably but ended in success.

Jacob had stolen his brother's blessing as the firstborn son. When brother Esau became exceedingly angry, Jacob had to leave his homeland. This trickster who stole his brother's birthright ended up traveling to the family's original homeland, being tricked himself, and working for his cousin Laban for fourteen years to gain the bride he really wanted. Jacob continued his life of trickery in Laban's land and eventually created enough bad feeling that he had to leave. On his way home, Jacob wrestled with God and seemed to gain wisdom, since that wrestling match ended his cunning ways. When he met his brother, Jacob acted deferentially toward him, and their disagreement was ended (Genesis 27–33).

The failure of the one-time trickster's life turned into victory as he fathered the children who became the basis for the Israelite nation. Jacob's change of heart turned his life around.

Jacob isn't alone in having a turning point with God. Chosen by God to rule His people, David seemed to have a terrific career ahead. But that career was deferred as he and King Saul battled for the throne.

As long as the challenges were great, David was faithful to his Lord. But this king was by no means perfect. After he gained the crown and life seemed to have settled down, faithfulness became a harder challenge. While his armies went out to war, David stayed in Jerusalem. One day from the roof of his home, he saw a beautiful woman bathing. Though Bathsheba was married to one of his soldiers, David had to have her. And in short order, this beauty was pregnant. Though David did all he could to try to make her husband, Uriah, think it was his child, he failed. Stymied, the king went to greater lengths to protect Bathsheba's reputation and had her husband killed.

That was not the last mistake in David's life, though it was the most personally disastrous. From that time on, peace did not rule in his household. Turmoil surrounded some of his children's lives. And toward the end of his days, David took a census of his people that displeased God and cost seventy thousand men's lives in the pestilence God used to punish Israel.

Despite all these failures, because the king repented, God still remembered that before He anointed David as king, He'd looked for a man after His own heart (1 Samuel 13:14), and the book of Acts declares that David was just that (Acts 13:22).

WHEN WE FAIL

The fact that we are sinners who fail daily has not escaped God's notice. The high opinion we often have of ourselves was never God's view of us anyway. "For all," He declares, "have sinned and fall short of the glory of God" (Romans 3:23 NKJV). God loves us despite our failures and sent His Son to be a picture of that love.

God loves us despite our failures and sent His Son to be a picture of that love.

Our perfection is not something we earn day by day. It was settled in eternity when Jesus died on the cross: "For by one sacrifice he has made perfect forever those who are being made holy" (Hebrews 10:14 NIV). Our good works are not a way for us to earn heaven; they are our way of showing God how much we love Him and are willing to serve Him. Nothing we could do would earn His great salvation, yet God is continuously at work, making us holy.

Frustrated by the weakness of his own body, the apostle Paul explained something He learned from God: "But he said to me, 'My grace is sufficient for you, for my power is made perfect in weakness.' Therefore I will boast all the more gladly about my weaknesses, so that Christ's power may rest on me" (2 Corinthians 12:9 NIV). God never expected us to be perfect; He simply wants us to be vessels His perfect Spirit can shine through (2 Corinthians 4:7).

We cannot excuse our failures or push them away, but we can recognize that whether it's a physical or moral failure, our right response is to turn to God and seek His help. Where forgiveness is needed, we must ask it; where we need wisdom, we can rely on Him for that, too (James 1:5). Then God's Spirit shines through us. What we cannot do is feel sorry for ourselves and throw in the towel.

Whether it's a physical or moral failure, our right response is to turn to God.

If God could make something of David and Jacob, He can work with us too. He has called us to walk with Him, and He remains next to us. In our personal doubts and questions, we only need to turn to Him.

After the Exodus, God promised His people an intimate relationship: "I will walk among you and be your God, and you will be my people" (Leviticus 26:12 NIV). Having fulfilled that promise in Jesus, who came to walk with us, can He ever be distant from us? Even in our failures, He will never walk away from us.

Remember, failure is only permanent in our earthly lives if we allow it to be. As long as God has us on this earth, there is hope for change—we can reverse our failure. And in eternity, if we have put our trust in Him, we cannot fail. He has promised it.

Can we be successful if we succeed in our own goals but fail in the goals that God has for us? Why or why not?

....

....

....

....

....

....

....

....

....

How can our faith in God help us through our personal failures?

....

....

....

....

....

....

....

....

How can we learn from Jacob's and David's
mistakes?

....

....

....

....

....

....

....

....

....

....

....

....

....

....

....

....

....

....

....

....

....

....

....

6
WHERE IS GOD
WHEN MONEY STRESSES ME OUT?

Whether you have a lot of money or very little, it can cause lots of stress. People with a lot of money often end up spending plenty of time deciding how to best invest it, and they may have many requests for money. Deciding how to make use of a lot is a different problem from not having enough to live on, but it bears a temptation those with little money rarely experience. Money can become so all-encompassing that people who have it begin to trust in it instead of in God.

Those without money may fall into the trap of worrying about the little they have and how to make it stretch far enough to sustain their lifestyle. In a harsh economy, that can be nearly a full-time challenge.

Whether we have plenty of cash or too little, because of our money situation, we can waste so many good things—both financial and otherwise—that God has given us. That's not how God meant our lives to be.

People have a lot of odd ideas about money.

People have a lot of odd ideas about money. First is the idea that it is evil. How many times have you heard someone say, "Money is the root of all evil"? They may not even know they are quoting the Bible—actually misquoting it. The Bible says,

"The *love of money* is the root of all evil: which while some coveted after, they have erred from the faith, and pierced themselves through with many sorrows" (1 Timothy 6:10 KJV, emphasis added). Money is not a living thing, and loving it is an inappropriate response. Scripture repeatedly calls on us to love one another (John 13:34–35; 15:2; Romans 12:10; 13:8; Galatians 5:13; 1 Thessalonians 3:12; 4:9), but it never tells us to love an inanimate object. Though we may say, "I love my car [home, clothes, or whatever]," when we do that we are not properly relating our feelings to God's Word. God gave us all those things to enjoy and use well, but not to love. That doesn't mean He doesn't want us to have lives that are rich with love, but it does mean He knows that worldly items cannot return our affections and will leave us empty in the end.

Use money to do good for people. Donate to your church, to parachurch organizations, or to your unbelieving neighbor who's short on money to feed her children. But don't turn it into a little green idol.

MONEY AND FAITH

Naturally no one in today's world physically bows down before a dollar bill or any other currency. But sometimes our attitudes toward money make it clear that we are quite fuzzy on what money means to us and how our use of it relates to our faith.

How we deal with money tells us a lot about how much we trust God. When we put our faith in our bank accounts instead of Him, trusting that they alone will see us through any troubles of the present or future, we have misunderstood who God is and what a frail support money can be. Scripture warns us: "Whoever loves money never has enough; whoever loves wealth is never satisfied with their income" (Ecclesiastes 5:10 NIV).

How we deal with money tells us a lot about how much we trust God.

When we look at our bank accounts to provide everything we need, we've forgotten that God has promised to provide for us. The prophet Joel reminded God's people who enabled them to reap their harvests: "Be glad then, you children of Zion, and rejoice in the LORD your God; for He has given you the former rain faithfully, and He will cause the rain to come down for you—the former rain, and the latter rain in the first month" (Joel 2:23 NKJV).

In an agrarian economy, the people would have understood that this meant God provided the regular rain that grew their crops. Just as we rely on a regular paycheck coming in, God's people in that age relied on rain that watered the seeds they'd worked hard to plant. No rain, no plants; good rain, good plants. When they received that blessing, they thanked God, whom they knew had provided for them.

We may not see as direct a connection between our workplace and God's provision, but it is He who gives us a job and keeps the company profitable enough for us to stay there. Though our bosses may not know Him, God may care for a company because some who know Him work there and because He has a purpose for that business. Though we may not see the direct connection between God and our "harvest," He is working to keep us working.

Even in financially tough times, God is tougher.

And when we lose a job and the economy is tough? Has God stopped caring? No. He has never forgotten one of His promises. And the author of Hebrews reminds us, "Let your conversation be without covetousness; and be content with such things as ye have: for he hath said, I will never leave thee, nor forsake thee" (Hebrews 13:5 KJV). Even in financially tough times when we can barely be content with what we have, God is tougher.

When those tough times come, as they do eventually, it's wise to take a look at our lives and check to see if we brought this upon ourselves by somehow missing the mark with our Lord. God may use a situation like this to get our attention. We should take a look at our financial lives and see if we have done careless spending, and of course we should consider what we have given. Have we held on to all our money, shortchanging God and the church? Were we tight with other people who could have expected better from us? If we carefully check our lives for all sin and can't identify anything, we might ask God to show us if we are missing something. Then we need to be open to His Spirit, who may show us a place in which we need to repent and redirect our lives.

But sometimes, even when we cannot find sin in our lives, the financial troubles (or other problems) remain. Look at Job, who kept insisting to his critical friends that he had not done something wrong that earned him all his woe. Job was serious about his spiritual life. Yet he recognized that he was not perfect and repented at the end of the book (Job 42:6). Still, nowhere does God criticize Job's sin to others, and He calls the sufferer's critical friends to repentance.

Sometimes, imperfect as we may be, God is not trying to get our attention because we've sinned but is trying to deepen our relationship with Him, as He did with Job. And that may mean we need to experience suffering. Though our Savior is extremely tender with us at many points in our lives, He has the ability to put us through hardship when that will be more to our long-term benefit. In such a case, though we may cry out to Him with questions and feel that we often don't get much of an answer to the issue that concerns us most, our relationship may remain tenderly close elsewhere. While our finances challenge us constantly, we may be growing spiritually; others may encourage us so kindly that we come to love them more deeply; our church life may seem especially blessed. *If only,* each of us may think, *this one part of my life weren't in crisis, things would be fine.* As time goes on, we may feel our spirits stretched to the max. But as we suffer these growing pains, we can be certain that God has not deserted us. And prayer can be our constant lifeline, connecting us with our Lord.

As we suffer growing pains, we can be certain that God has not deserted us.

WEALTH AND FAITH

But what of those who have plenty of money? Are they closer to God than the poor? Not necessarily. For money disconnected from the knowledge of God brings no great spiritual value. Moses warned God's prosperous people: "You may say to yourself, 'My power and the strength of my hands have produced this wealth for me.' But remember the LORD your God, for it is he who gives you the ability to produce wealth, and so confirms his covenant, which he swore to your ancestors, as it is today" (Deuteronomy 8:17–18 NIV).

Whether we have much or little, we owe it to our Lord. In 1 Samuel 2:7 (NIV) Hannah prayed: "The LORD sends poverty and wealth; he humbles and he exalts." Money cannot vie with God, when it comes to providing physical security, nor can it provide the love of others that gives emotional security.

Whether we have much or little, we owe it to our Lord.

When God gives us extra, gratitude is the appropriate response, and we need to use that spare cash wisely.

Job's description of a wealthy wicked man highlights the need for people to look in the right place for their security:

Though he heaps up silver like dust
and clothes like piles of clay,
what he lays up the righteous will wear,
and the innocent will divide his silver.
The house he builds is like a moth's cocoon,
like a hut made by a watchman.
He lies down wealthy,
but will do so no more;
when he opens his eyes, all is gone.
Terrors overtake him like a flood;
a tempest snatches him away in the night.
The east wind carries him off,
and he is gone;
it sweeps him out of his place.

Job 27:16–21 NIV

Without God, the world is an insecure place. And money can only do so much to lend security to it. More often, it leads us to put our trust in the wrong place, and soon we find our lives strangely empty.

While we assume money can solve any problem, scripture points us to other things that may be of greater benefit. For example, "Wisdom is a shelter as money is a shelter, but the advantage of knowledge is this: Wisdom preserves those who have it" (Ecclesiastes 7:12 NIV).

Finding the Way to Security

One thing we need not do if we face financial limitations is become jealous of those who seem to profit while we are struggling to make ends meet. Mere earthly riches cannot compare to the blessings God willingly provides to His servants: "The blessing of the LORD makes one rich, and He adds no sorrow with it" (Proverbs 10:22 NKJV). God calls us to receive greater riches than the bills or coins that quickly leave us and land in someone else's pockets.

"Is anyone thirsty?
Come and drink—even if you have no money!
Come, take your choice of wine or milk—
it's all free!
Why spend your money on food
that does not give you strength?
Why pay for food that does you no good?
Listen to me, and you will eat what is good.
You will enjoy the finest food.
Come to me with your ears wide open.
Listen, and you will find life.
I will make an everlasting covenant with you.
I will give you all the unfailing love
I promised to David."
ISAIAH 55:1–3 NLT

Ultimately, wealth will not give anyone God's blessings in eternity: "Why should I fear when trouble comes, when enemies surround me? They trust in their wealth and boast of great riches. Yet they cannot redeem themselves from death by paying a ransom to God" (Psalm 49:5–7 NLT). The ransom can only be paid by Jesus.

God reminds us that life is more than a paycheck, investments, or a retirement fund. While we tend to think of blessings as the things we own, He would have us see a larger picture. When God speaks of blessings, he may or may not mean anything financial. There are many elements to life that have nothing to do with money.

Life is more than a paycheck, investments, or a retirement fund.

When we get confused about money and God, we open ourselves to danger. Jesus warned us: "No one can serve two masters; for either he will hate the one and love the other, or else he will be loyal to the one and despise the other. You cannot serve God and mammon" (Matthew 6:24 NKJV). We need to choose whom we serve.

Those who have money should use it in a way

that pleases the Lord. There are benefits to not holding onto worldly riches that provide both eternal and practical gain. "[The one]who lends money to the poor without interest. . .will never be shaken" (Psalm 15:5 NIV). No matter how much money we have in the bank, God promises: "Give, and it shall be given unto you; good measure, pressed down, and shaken together, and running over, shall men give into your bosom. For with the same measure that ye mete withal it shall be measured to you again" (Luke 6:38 KJV) and, "The generous soul will be made rich, and he who waters will also be watered himself" (Proverbs 11:25 NKJV). There is no specific description of the kind of generosity or what the believer is watering with, but where God has blessed people with a good financial base, certainly it's to be expected that would be part of the generosity. Giving to a church is great place to start, but sharing what we have need not end there. God has put us in this world to help others. And wherever He calls us to give, we should be ready to help.

God has put us in this world to help others.

And in case we think we might do something less than aboveboard with our money, God warns:

"Dishonest money dwindles away, but whoever gathers money little by little makes it grow" (Proverbs 13:11 NIV).

Scripture has much to say about money, and none of it encourages us to cling to or trust in it. One of the greatest approbations Jesus gave anyone was a woman who was so down and out that, perhaps in desperation, she put all her money into the temple offering.

Jesus sat down opposite the place where the offerings were put and watched the crowd
putting their money into the temple treasury.
Many rich people threw in large amounts.
But a poor widow came and put in two very small copper coins, worth only a few cents.
Calling his disciples to him, Jesus said,
"Truly I tell you, this poor widow has put more into the treasury than all the others. They all gave out of their wealth; but she, out of her poverty, put in everything—all she had to live on."
MARK 12:41–44 NIV

The thought of putting all our money into God's hands may terrify us, but can we have any doubt that God not only saw this woman's situation but also did something about it? It is the same for us. When we cast our financial cares on Him and seek His answers, He may not provide us with a million dollars, but He will provide. He has promised. In Matthew 6, after warning that no one can serve two masters, Jesus called on his disciples not to take thought of what they ate or drank or wore. Then he pointed them to the birds and the lilies of the field, for whom God provides, and ended with the words, "But seek ye first the kingdom of God, and his righteousness; and all these things shall be added unto you" (vv. 25–33 KJV).

Let's get God's message: When we took look to Him in our financial dealings, we have nothing to fear.

Do you consider financial success to be a blessing? If so, what responsibilities come with such a blessing?

....
....
....
....
....
....
....
....
....

How does our attitude toward money relate to our relationship with God?

....
....
....
....
....
....
....
....
....

How important is it to trust God in financial matters?

7
WHERE IS GOD
WHEN THE FUTURE LOOKS DIM?

Have you looked into the future and found it a bleak prospect? It doesn't matter if you've faced one overwhelming problem or a collection of smaller troubles that combined into a perfect storm of fear. Looking into the future without hope is a discouraging situation.

TEMPTATIONS BEFORE US

Fear of the future has been one of the great temptations Satan has always used against Christians. After all, even when we live well-ordered lives, we really don't know what's ahead of us. We understand that disasters strike people, even good and faithful ones. And in our ever-changing world, challenges in our culture and economy constantly arise. Human society has no firm bedrock to stand on, and flux is its constant state of being.

Human society has no firm bedrock to stand on.

Only God can become the firm foundation for our home lives, church relationships, workplace interactions, and our society at large. But in some of these places, Christianity is less than welcome. We don't live in a Christian world, so as we interact with others we can have a battle before us to keep our thoughts as positive as they need to be. There's always someone to spread the doom and gloom when life is looking less than pleasant.

Once Satan reminds us of the constant load of troubles this world bears and gets our minds off our Savior and onto the future, he has great success in leading us into worry. C. S. Lewis recognized this in his book *The Screwtape Letters*, which depicts a senior demon training a new one. Advising his student demon on tempting his subject, Screwtape says:

> Our business is to get [humans] away from the eternal, and from the Present. . . .
> It is far better to make them live in the Future. Biological necessity makes all their passions point in that direction already, so that thought about the Future inflames hope and fear. Also, it is unknown to them, so that in making them think about it we make them think of unrealities. In a word, the Future is, of all things, the thing least like eternity. It is the most completely temporal part of time.

How do we respond to a life in which we seem to be living with our feet firmly in the air? Looking toward the future, we become aware of the frailty of our own beings. Though this is nothing new to us— we have known all along that our bodies have a use-by date—suddenly it impacts our thoughts and fears, and that date becomes a painful reality. At this point we have a choice before us, an opportunity to choose where we put our trust.

Where we put that trust is a decision every one of us needs to make, not once but throughout our lives. If we've been Christians for more than a very short time, our minds know the right answer. But so often, other options look so much more tempting, and even if we have read the scriptures and know God is our only hope, we can be drawn elsewhere, perhaps down a path that looks easier. Or, if doubt has already ferreted into our hearts and made us fear that God could leave us in the lurch, the tempter's job is done.

TEMPTED IN OTHER DIRECTIONS

Because fear for the future pulls so strongly at our hearts and waiting on God can be such a challenge, the temptation to put our trust in other people can be strong. We may begin in the firm determination

> *The temptation to put our trust in other people can be strong.*

to cling to our Lord, but as challenges arise, we find ourselves slipping just a bit. If doubt fills our hearts, we may suddenly become eager to cling to anyone who promises a brighter tomorrow.

Maybe that's why, in a day when our society prides itself on scientific knowledge and the ability to know what is real and what isn't, many people, including some Christians, persist in consulting psychics and others who claim to know what lies ahead. This despite the fact that God specifically warns His people against such practices (Leviticus 19:31; 20:6, 27; Isaiah 8:19), and putting trust in them puts us at great risk spiritually, since they slowly and smoothly draw us away from Him. Finally we are likely to discover that such attempts to circumvent God will not be successful, since other people cannot know the future any more than we do (Ecclesiastes 8:7).

Modern-day believers aren't the only ones who have fallen into this trap. Ancient Israel had its own variation on that story in a long history of listening to the prophet who offered the most pleasing news.

Often that meant they ignored the prophet with God's real message. Moses warned against turning to false prophets who titillate our senses, and explained the danger:

> *"Suppose there are prophets among you*
> *or those who dream dreams about the*
> *future, and they promise you signs*
> *or miracles, and the predicted signs*
> *or miracles occur. If they then say,*
> *'Come, let us worship other gods'—gods*
> *you have not known before—do not listen*
> *to them. The Lord your God*
> *is testing you to see if you truly love*
> *him with all your heart and soul."*
> DEUTERONOMY 13:1–3 NLT

But facing a test doesn't mean we have to give in to temptation.

THE CHALLENGE TO FAITH

When we face the what-ifs of the future, whether they be far distant moments or just a day or two away, we easily become anxious about our own frailty. Some things we can prepare for, to ease any trauma in our lives, but others are completely beyond our control. Most nerve-wracking are the unexpected dramas that suddenly fall into our lives—physical disasters that once seemed so distant of us and now have parked themselves on our doorsteps, economic situations that seem out of control of even the wisest government leaders, a cultural rift that seems beyond the ability of humans to deal with and constantly causes social stress. The doubts these events create concerning our safety may feel very real to us, even if they are actually never part of our futures. Like Chicken Little, we run about feeling confident the sky is falling.

We run about feeling confident the sky is falling.

But it doesn't even take a traumatic development to make the future look scary. When we face any kind of change, even a good one, it may cause us to stop and think. Fears for unknown dangers ahead may make us step back from a good thing God has in mind for us, whether it be a new job, a ministry opportunity, or a change in our relationships.

When Amy Carmichael planned to go into missionary work, she admitted:

I had feelings of fear about the future. . . .
The devil kept on whispering, "It's all right
now, but what about afterward? You are
going to be very lonely" . . . And I turned
to my God in a kind of desperation and
said "Lord, what can I do? How can I go
on to the end?" And He said, "None of
them that trust in Me shall be desolate."
That word has been with me ever since.

Whatever lies before us, one constant problem remains in our lives: The future always presents a challenge to faith. We will never, in this life, be able to look down time and see exactly where our paths will take us. And sometimes that's a good thing, since knowing the troubles we'd walk through could be very frightening. God allows enough turns in the road that we cannot see the whole path He will have us tread. But we can take heart, knowing that He is making every turn with us.

WHAT DO WE REALLY FEAR?

When vague fears for the future attack us, it may be helpful to identify where our anxiety lies. Perhaps we fear something that will never happen. After all, look back at your life and see what you worried about that never came to pass. Was it that you'd never marry or never be happy in your marriage? Perhaps today you are blessed in your relationship with your spouse. Or maybe you feared God would ask you to become a missionary in some dangerous country, but instead He gave you a ministry in your own backyard. Our fears are rarely based on reality.

Our fears are rarely based on reality.

Or maybe we've been afraid of other people? God specifically tells us we need not fear the wicked, when they come against us, for in the end, He will prosper His people. David reflects this hope for our futures when he says, "Consider the blameless, observe the upright; a future awaits those who seek peace. But all sinners will be destroyed; there will be no future for the wicked" (Psalm 37:37–38 NIV). And the book of Proverbs both warns and promises: "Do not let your heart envy sinners, but always be zealous for the fear of the LORD. There is surely a future hope for you, and your hope will not be cut off" (Proverbs 23:17–19 NIV). God looks after His faithful people and shows them a way of hope. He also uses them to reach out to those sinners and draw them into His embrace.

As fears begin to well up, remember that nothing we go through in life surprises God. He has known about our situations all along and has prepared us for them. Though every moment of our future days may not be pleasant, all head in a positive direction if we are trusting in our Maker. He has a heavenly goal in mind for us—salvation. And he promises, "I am Alpha and Omega, the beginning and the end. I will give unto him that is athirst of the fountain of the water of life freely" (Revelation 21:6 KJV). He has been around for all of creation and knows all there is to know about our world. Nothing escapes God, from the smallest trouble in our lives to the largest ones of our world.

Nothing escapes God, from the smallest trouble in our lives to the largest ones of our world.

Do we fear what God will do in our lives? "Weak Christians are afraid of the shadow of the cross," commented Puritan preacher Thomas Brooks, a man who was no stranger to trial, since he lived during the bloody and divisive English Civil War and stayed in London with his congregation through that city's devastating Great Plague of 1665. All of us at some point feel trepidation about the suffering that comes with carrying our crosses. While we fear those trials, God is trying to build us into more powerful believers—people who can amaze the world with the things they do through Christ's empowering Spirit. But we cannot have that kind of future if we constantly back down from the cross when He puts it into our lives.

If we doubt God's good intentions toward us, let's remember that when God's disobedient people had been conquered and were headed to Babylon, He gave them this promise:

> *This is what the LORD says:*
> *"When seventy years are completed*
> *for Babylon, I will come to you and*
> *fulfill my good promise*
> *to bring you back to this place.*
> *For I know the plans I have for you,"*
> *declares the LORD, "plans to*
> *prosper you and not to harm you,*
> *plans to give you hope and a future.*
> *Then you will call on me and come*
> *and pray to me, and I will listen to you."*
> JEREMIAH 29:10–12 NIV

Many trials and troubles may touch our lives, but none last forever. If we use them as an opportunity to turn to God and learn more of Him, He will use hard times to bring us blessing. Our hope for the future lies with God, and when we call on Him and really mean it, He will hear.

How does fear of the future affect our lives?

....
....
....
....
....
....
....
....
....
....

How does fear of the unkown impact our day-to-day actions? How does it impact our relationship with God?

....
....
....
....
....
....
....
....
....
....

Do you ever fear what God might do in your life?
Is this spiritually healthy? Why or why not?

8
WHERE IS GOD
WHEN THE WORLD SEEMS CRAZY?

"You will hear of wars and rumors of wars. . . . Nation will rise against nation, and kingdom against kingdom. There will be famines and earthquakes in various places." This description in Matthew 24:6–7 (NIV) fairly accurately describe the world scene today, doesn't it? With wars rising up in places we'd never heard of and the threat of even more conflicts barely being forestalled, with terrorism at a new high, we often seem to live on a knife-edge, nervous and awaiting one final traumatic event. And even when war doesn't threaten us, our unpredictable world does, with natural disasters affecting even the most unexpected places. The world is a dangerous place in which to live.

The world is a dangerous place in which to live.

But the missing part of that first verse says: "But see to it that you are not alarmed. Such things must happen, but the end is still to come." On reading that, we give a sigh of relief and feel as if we can live another day—that is, if this is not the end that verse speaks of.

THREATS ON EVERY SIDE

The good news is that this is not the first time in the history of God's people that wars devastated their country and threats came from every side. Throughout history, believers have faced such problems, and God has a history of helping His people, no matter how things seem to be stacked against them.

The land God gave the Jews lies in a very important spot; in the days of the prophets, Israel was a key trade-route area, and many kings coveted it. In ancient history, the Egyptians, Assyrians, Babylonians, Greeks, and Romans wanted to own this turf. All made efforts to add it to their kingdoms—and all but Egypt did so successfully. Peace has always been elusive in the country of God's people.

The situation hasn't changed much for the Holy Land throughout the centuries. In the twentieth and twenty-first centuries one small but critical nation has been a toehold for her people, despite Israel's being surrounded by enemies. Surprisingly—at least to her enemies—none of them have managed to dislodge the Jews, who have nowhere else to go. Nowhere, that is, except to God, for He is the One who promised the land to them and has kept that promise.

From the time when God initially gave that land to His people, the battles have been fierce. At the head of His first fighting force, God placed Joshua, one of the two faithful spies whom He had sent into the Holy Land forty years before. Though he'd spent forty years wandering in the desert, Joshua was still confident that Israel could conquer the land God set before them.

The reason for Joshua's confidence and courage? It had nothing to do with well-trained warriors (Joshua didn't have any) or up-to-date battle equipment (there was little enough of that on the side of the Israelites). Joshua and his soldiers depended on God for their victories. And as unlikely as it seemed, with some hard fighting and some unusual tactics, they destroyed their enemies' cities.

Joshua and his soldiers depended on God for their victories.

When Joshua died, Israel had yet to conquer much of the Promised Land. But God told His warrior-leader that He Himself would drive out the enemies (Joshua 13:6). Despite the seemingly impossible odds, by the time of kings David and Solomon, Israel controlled that land.

The world has always been crazy, and God's people have often been in the thick of it, but no matter what they faced, God stood with them and brought them through. What He did in the past, He can do today, too.

TODAY'S CRAZY WORLD

For all the technology that fills our world, war has not improved things since the time of Joshua. GPS-empowered cell phones, drones, and cutting-edge planes and tanks have not ended war, just made it more deadly. And war is only the beginning. As people find new ways to harm each other, our world seems increasingly ungovernable. Our faith in politicians and other world leaders wanes as world events seem more and more unpredictable. And as we've begun to see more natural disasters ruin our cities and climate change alter the places we live in, it seems as if no one may be immune to trouble. Life is out of control on this planet—everything seems to have become crazy.

The solution to our fears for a crazy world—whether one where man tries to destroy man or where the whole world itself seems to revolt—has not changed. Joshua's confidence can be ours too. "Do not be afraid of sudden terror," the book of Proverbs commands us, "nor of trouble from the wicked when it comes; for the LORD will be your confidence, and will keep your foot from being caught" (Proverbs 3:25–26

NKJV). Our confidence and courage come from the same place Joshua's did. And just as God saved him and his people by amazing methods, He can reach into our lives to bring us through the most bizarre threats.

If you've been a Christian for long, you've probably had days when you expected disaster, but in response to prayer God brought some change in your life that turned it all around. One moment you had an unsolvable problem; shortly thereafter, everything was fine because of God's intervention. That almost seems to be a signature of God's work in our lives. It's as if a small miracle reminds us that God has not forgotten us. And that may be just what happens. For when we are faithful (and sometimes even when we are not), God is guarding and guiding us.

When we are faithful (and sometimes even when we are not), God is guarding and guiding us.

During trials, one psalmist recognized the importance of two responses to trouble: faithfulness to God and the need to stick close to Him, through His Word. "Many are my persecutors and my enemies, yet I do not turn from Your testimonies. I see the treacherous, and am disgusted, because they do not keep Your word. Consider how I love Your precepts; revive me, O LORD, according to Your lovingkindness. The entirety of Your word is truth, and every one of Your righteous judgments endures forever" (Psalm 119:157–60 NKJV). When we respond this way, we are constantly available to hear His guidance and seek His protection.

The psalmist offers excellent advice, since God's Word both comforts us and provides direction. How many times have you barely known how to go on, and when you picked up your Bible, its words jumped out at you with encouragement or the guidance you needed? God is so intimately connected with us that He often provides us with direction this way, if we have made it a habit to remain in His Word daily. But if we will not make it a habit, we may pick up the Word only to have it feel barren and empty. God takes it very seriously when we fail to commune with Him through prayer and His Word.

David, one of Israel's greatest kings, who led a tumultuous and dangerous life, knew where to put his trust whether he was in the middle of battle or in the midst of a family dispute. He declared: "But as for me, I trust in You, O LORD; I say, 'You are my God.' My times are in Your hand; deliver me from the hand of my enemies, and from those who persecute me" (Psalm 31:14–15 NKJV). Though it may be easy to feel that the idea of turning to God in trial is a mere platitude, David knew otherwise. Often, trusting in God is the spiritual battle that comes before or after the physical one. It takes strength to put our faith in God when we feel overwhelmed by troubles. Satan is likely to whisper in our ears, "That's no solution. Better to take things into your own hands!" If we're not alert, we may give in to the temptation to act immediately and may fail to do what God often asks of us: to wait.

Scripture often encourages us to wait on God when we face a troubling situation.

Scripture often encourages us to wait on God when we face a troubling situation. David, who must often have waited for perfect battle timing and had to encourage his soldiers to do the same, counsels us, "Wait on the LORD: be of good courage, and he shall strengthen thine heart: wait, I say, on the LORD" (Psalm 27:14 KJV). And his wise son, Solomon, advised, "Say not thou, I will recompense evil; but wait on the LORD, and he shall save thee" (Proverbs 20:22 KJV). We need not rush to straighten out confused situations before we take counsel of God. He judges all things correctly and brings about His perfect justice. He who is "the habitation of justice" will always see that right is done, whether it comes in this life or in eternity (Jeremiah 50:7 KJV). Though His timing may not always suit our internal clocks, God will never be late or forgetful.

God gives a wonderful promise to those who wait: "But they that wait upon the LORD shall renew their strength; they shall mount up with wings as eagles; they shall run, and not be weary; and they shall walk, and not faint" (Isaiah 40:31 KJV).

Waiting requires us to develop our trust that God really will take action. Instead of responding in our own hectic manner, God calls on us to relax and let Him take control. Kindly, He counters our nervousness with this promise with a warning attached: "Behold, the LORD's hand is not shortened, that it cannot save; nor His ear heavy, that it cannot hear. But your iniquities have separated you from your God; and your sins have hidden His face from you, so that He will not hear" (Isaiah 59:1–2 NKJV). As we trust in Him and confess our own wrongdoing, His salvation appears before us.

And when we fear because the weather or the land seems so unpredictable, God asks us, "Who is in control of the earth?" Job reminded His critics:

> *He moves mountains without their knowing it*
> *and overturns them in his anger.*
> *He shakes the earth from its place*
> *and makes its pillars tremble.*
> *He speaks to the sun and it does not shine;*
> *he seals off the light of the stars.*
> *He alone stretches out the heavens*
> *and treads on the waves of the sea.*
> *He is the Maker of the Bear and Orion,*
> *the Pleiades and the constellations of the south.*
> *He performs wonders that cannot be fathomed,*
> *miracles that cannot be counted.*
>
> JOB 9:5–10 NIV

RESPONSE TO A CRAZY WORLD

He who created the world is in control of it and our lives. Even if a natural disaster affects us, can He not bring good out of that? For wherever we go, He is, too (Hebrews 13:5). No natural disaster separates us from Him, unless we despair of His help and turn from Him. Even our struggles bring blessing, if we cling to Him throughout them.

When we fear storms or other dangers, it is

prayer time. As we lift our needs and the needs of our neighbors up to God, He hears and answers according to His will. "Do not be anxious about anything, but in every situation, by prayer and petition, with thanksgiving, present your requests to God," God's Word tells us, but it also gives us a promise: "And the peace of God, which transcends all understanding, will guard your hearts and your minds in Christ Jesus" (Philippians 4:6–7 KJV). Whether or not we realize it, our peace lies not in the things we own or the good experiences we have, but in our Lord. When He stands by us in the fight or storm, we stand in the center of His peace.

> *When we fear storms or other dangers, it is prayer time.*

"God incarnate is the end of fear; and the heart that realizes that He is in the midst. . .will be quiet in the middle of alarm" is the way F. B. Meyer explained this.

When we live in that kind of peace, no pain on earth can harm us forever.

Do you ever fear the craziness of today's world? What role can faith in God play in alleviating this fear?

....

....

....

....

....

....

....

....

....

....

....

....

....

....

....

....

....

....

....

....

....

....

How can communing with God provide direction in troubled times?

Why is it important that we "wait on the Lord"?

9
WHERE IS GOD WHEN MY HEALTH IS FAILING?

One day, most of us will experience the intimate betrayal of our own bodies. When we least expect it, some physical ailment will strike, and suddenly we will realize that we are not physically invincible. Maybe our health will be seriously compromised, and we will begin thinking of eternity with new intensity.

As hard as we try to take care of our physical beings, we cannot live forever on this earth. Though God promises us many things, eternal life on earth is not among them.

But even when our bodies fail us, our Lord does not. God is never distant from us and never stops caring for us physically or spiritually. Nothing about our physical beings lies beyond His power. "What is the price of two sparrows—one copper coin?" Jesus asked His disciples. Then He added, "But not a single sparrow can fall to the ground without your Father knowing it. And the very hairs on your head are all numbered. So don't be afraid; you are more valuable to God than a whole flock of sparrows" (Matthew 10:29–31 NLT). He knows everything we are going through and will not leave or forsake us, no matter

> *Even when our bodies fail us, our Lord does not.*

what happens (Hebrews 13:5).

Mark 5:25–34 tells the story of one woman whose suffering had gone on for twelve years. Though she had visited many doctors and spent all her money to pay them, her constant bleeding problem remained with her and had even gotten worse.

Then she heard about Jesus. Here was someone who might help. It seems as if He was her last hope, and she determinedly clung to it. She came to Him when He was surrounded by a crowd of people. To get his attention long enough to receive a healing must have seemed impossible, but this woman never failed in her trust. "If I can just touch his robe, I will be healed," she told herself (v. 28 NLT). She was humble enough not to need a face-to-face meeting with the Lord. Even the simplest connection would do for her. As she courageously reached out and touched the Savior's robe, her bleeding stopped in an instant. She had been right—she was completely healed just by touching Jesus.

Recognizing that the woman had received His power, Jesus turned to find out who had touched Him. With such a crowd around Him, the disciples couldn't believe He was serious. How could he know that one person had touched Him with more than a simple brush of a hand? Didn't the crowd pack about Him?

Just then, trembling at the understanding of

what had just happened to her, the woman came close and fell on her knees before Him.

"Daughter," Jesus gently told her, "your faith has made you well. Go in peace. Your suffering is over" (v. 34 NLT). How she must have rejoiced that day, not only at the joy of meeting Jesus, her Savior, but also at the miraculous work He'd done in her life.

Throughout the scriptures, God makes it clear He is intimately involved in health and healing. It is His touch that brings healing to our lives, both spiritually and physically. Faith and healing are deeply connected. Proverbs 3:7–8 (NKJV) warns and promises us: "Do not be wise in your own eyes; fear the Lord and depart from evil. It will be health to your flesh, and strength to your bones." The book of Proverbs repeatedly connects our spiritual and physical health (see, for example, Proverbs 14:30; 17:22).

Faith and healing are deeply connected.

Scripture shows an intimate relationship between those people who are healed and the God who heals them. These are not fly-by incidents between Jesus and some strange but hurting people; the ones who receive healing have faith in Him.

Though God may have mercy on unbelievers or those who have lapsed in their faith, for believing Christians, intimacy with God cannot be separated from physical healing. When we are walking close to Him, we are in a place where healing can happen. Following the Exodus, God promised His people, "If you diligently heed the voice of the LORD your God and do what is right in His sight, give ear to His commandments and keep all His statutes, I will put none of the diseases on you which I have brought on the Egyptians. For I am the LORD who heals you" (Exodus 15:26 NKJV). And physical healing doubtless is connected with the delicate work the Spirit does within the heart of the one who is healed.

It's hardly surprising God would make that kind of spiritual connection between the body and soul, when His own Son gave His body for us. The apostle Peter described this connection when he spoke of Jesus as He "who Himself bore our sins in His own body on the tree, that we, having died to sins, might live for righteousness—by whose stripes you were healed" (1 Peter 2:24 NKJV).

Much as we might not like to admit it, there is also some connection between illness and sin on our side, too. Whether we have a bad habit, like smoking, that affects our hearts and pulmonary system, or we are innocently affected by something in our environment, this world impacts the delicate body God gave us. And that finely tuned organism may also react to our ongoing sin with physical symptoms.

When Jesus came to his adopted hometown, Capernaum, Mark 2:1–12 tells us He spoke to a packed crowd. As He preached, some men brought a paralyzed man up onto the roof, dug through the roof, and dropped the man nearly into Jesus' lap. Immediately, Jesus identified the problem. "Son, your sins are forgiven," he told the man (v. 5 NIV). Some of the teachers of the law immediately objected, saying that only God could forgive sins. So to prove the truth of that, Jesus responded, " 'Which is easier: to say to this paralyzed man, "Your sins are forgiven," or to say, "Get up, take your mat and walk"? But I want you to know that the Son of Man has authority on earth to forgive sins.' So he said to the man, 'I tell you, get up, take your mat and go home' " (vv. 9–11 NIV). The man rose, picked up his mat, and walked away from both his sins and paralysis, leaving a praise fest behind him.

This world impacts the delicate body God gave us.

And the apostle James described the way the New Testament church was to help a sufferer.

Is anyone among you sick? Let them call the elders of the church to pray over them and anoint them with oil in the name of the Lord. And the prayer offered in faith will make the sick person well; the Lord will raise them up. If they have sinned, they will be forgiven. Therefore confess your sins to each other and pray for each other so that you may be healed. The prayer of a righteous person is powerful and effective.
JAMES 5:14–16 NIV

But it's noticeable that though Jesus confronted this man and others with their sins as He healed them, He does not always do so, and in his letter James indicates only the possibility that sin may be the problem behind an illness. In the case of the woman with the bleeding problem, Jesus commended her instead of pointing out sin. So it's unreasonable to say that all physical ailments are caused by a sufferer's sin, as some would claim. Scripture doesn't testify to that, so neither should we. Instead, we need to trust that God works in all situations and can direct each person to confess and turn away from sin or simply trust in Him. God works in every heart individually and does not need people to critique others who are already hurting.

David experienced healing and cried out in praise, "O Lord my God, I cried out to You, and You healed me" (Psalm 30:2 NKJV).

When we're ill, we need to follow David's example and pray for healing. God wants to respond to our requests in this area as in others. And He has the power to bring us back to health. But before asking for physical wholeness, wise believers will bring wrongdoings or failures before God in confession and seek to do His will so that a bad spiritual life will not interfere with a return to health. And many have found that when they need to make changes that lead to health, God provides them with the strength to do so.

God does not need people to critique others who are already hurting.

But prayer does not stop with confession and a request for God to remove illness from us. Often the healing God puts in place is not instantaneous. That's when Christians need to remain faithful in prayer. For

God does not always heal in a moment, but He will always support us when our bodies are working less than optimally. And as pains and weakness afflict us, our spirits may feel rather worn. Drawing near God can strengthen and heal them, too.

While we pray, we should also make the best use we can of doctors who may ease our pain or bring healing through medication and medical procedures. The woman with a bleeding problem did not avoid the doctors. She had had the best care available to her. And nowhere in scripture does God tell us to avoid such earthly care. Instead, we can make use of the good God has made available in the medical community at the same time as we seek a spiritual solution. Between these two, many ailments and diseases can be cured.

IF GOD DOES NOT HEAL

We'd like to think that God would heal every faithful Christian of every ailment. But it didn't happen during the first century, and it does not happen today. The most prominent example of an unhealed Christian in scripture is the apostle Paul, who testified in 2 Corinthians 12: "There was given to me a thorn in the flesh, the messenger of Satan to buffet me, lest I should be exalted above measure" (2:7 KJV). Three times Paul asked God to remove this ailment, but the Savior replied, "My grace is sufficient for thee: for my strength is made perfect in weakness" (v. 9 KJV). Not exactly the answer Paul was hoping for. But the apostle concluded that Jesus could work through this, too, as his attitude after receiving this news shows: "Most gladly therefore will I rather glory in my infirmities, that the power of Christ may rest upon me. Therefore I take pleasure in infirmities, in reproaches, in necessities, in persecutions, in distresses for Christ's sake: for when I am weak, then am I strong" (vv. 9–10 KJV).

In the same epistle, Paul describes the relationship of our bodies to the Spirit's work within them: "But we have this treasure in earthen vessels, that the excellence of the power may be of God and not of us" (2 Corinthians 4:7 NKJV).

Though we may not relish a lack of healing in our lives, we can find joy in the work God still does through us. Perhaps our greatest testimonies will come when we are weakest and retain a deep faith in our Lord. For when God does not heal, He can still work with great

When God does not heal, He can still work with great power in our lives.

power in our lives as His light shines out of broken earthen vessels.

And what if that illness takes our lives? Paul has an answer for that, too. He points us toward the eternity we will share with our Lord:

> *Therefore we do not lose heart.*
> *Even though our outward man is*
> *perishing, yet the inward man is being*
> *renewed day by day. For our light*
> *affliction, which is but for a moment, is*
> *working for us a far more exceeding and*
> *eternal weight of glory, while we do not*
> *look at the things which are seen, but*
> *at the things which are not seen. For the*
> *things which are seen are temporary, but*
> *the things which are not seen are eternal.*
> 2 Corinthians 4:16–18 nkjv

When our outward being perishes, there is still more to come. We leave this earth, suffering is past, and we are at home in Jesus.

How is our spiritual health conncted to our physical health?

....
....
....
....
....
....
....
....
....
....

Why is it mportant to confess our sins before praying for healing?

....
....
....
....
....
....
....
....
....

How can physical ailments affect our relationship with God?

How can we comfort those who have lost loved ones to illness?

10

WHERE IS GOD?
HE IS ALWAYS WITH YOU

Life can overwhelm us. As we look around us, doubts and fears assail us, and if we are faced with fears for long, we may wonder where God is in our trials.

Somehow many Christians have gotten the false idea that troubles should never happen to faithful believers, but scripture tells us otherwise. Trials and tribulations can be the very things that make our faith shine brightly. The apostle Paul, instead of questioning God, grabbed onto tribulations as opportunities to shine for Christ: "But we glory in tribulations also: knowing that tribulation worketh patience; and patience, experience; and experience, hope: and hope maketh not ashamed; because the love of God is shed abroad in our hearts by the Holy Ghost which is given unto us" (Romans 5:3–5 KJV). The apostle leapt into the spiritual battle and used it as an opportunity to reach others for Christ.

Trials and tribulations can be the very things that make our faith shine brightly.

Even though his troubles were not resolved, Paul remained faithful and testified: "We are pressed on every side by troubles, but we are not crushed. We are perplexed, but not driven to despair. We are hunted down, but never abandoned by God. We get knocked down, but we are not destroyed. Through suffering, our bodies continue to share in the death of Jesus so that the life of Jesus may also be seen in our bodies" (2 Corinthians 4:8–10 NLT). For the apostle, everything pointed back to Jesus and the message He had given him to share with the world.

WHEN GOD SEEMS SILENT

Has God seemed to desert you? Impossible (Hebrews 13:5). God is not a bad father, who leaves His children when things get tough. A. W. Tozer said: "We need never shout across the spaces to an absent God. He is nearer than our own soul, closer than our most secret thoughts." The problem, when we doubt His love, is never that He has stopped loving us. Though we may need to wait for Him, we need never doubt His love and protection.

"But you, O LORD, are a shield around me," David declared. "You are my glory, the one who holds my head high. I cried out to the LORD, and he answered me from his holy mountain" (Psalm 3:3–4 NLT). This testimony comes from the man who had been promised he would be king of Israel but had to wait for many years to receive the crown. Even when it did seem God's promise would come true, it did not happen overnight. First David was anointed king of Judah (2 Samuel 2:4). But Saul's son Ish-Bosheth was made king over Israel and reigned two years before some of his own men murdered him. David, instead of rejoicing that the crown would be his, was concerned that the murderers of an innocent man should be punished (2 Samuel 2:8–10; 4).

We must never stop communicating with God in the midst of our fears. Like the prophet, in times of trouble we may cry out: "LORD, be gracious to us; we long for you. Be our strength every morning, our salvation in time of distress" (Isaiah 33:3 NIV). Who else can we go to when fears assault us? Where on earth is there an answer?

> *We must never stop communicating with God in the midst of our fears.*

Just as Paul gloried in tribulations, he knew where to go for help and comfort: "Praise be to the God and Father of our Lord Jesus Christ, the Father of compassion and the God of all comfort, who comforts us in all our troubles. . . . For just as we share abundantly in the sufferings of Christ, so also our comfort abounds through Christ" (2 Corinthians 1:3–5 NIV).

Both men had a response to fear: trust in God. And over and over David repeatedly shared the importance of that trust in the Psalms:

Those who know your name trust in you,
for you, LORD, have never forsaken
those who seek you.
PSALM 9:10 NIV

Some trust in chariots and some in horses,
but we trust in the name
of the LORD our God.
PSALM 20:7 NIV

I have heard the many rumors about
me, and I am surrounded by terror. My
enemies conspire against me, plotting
to take my life. But I am trusting you, O
LORD, saying, "You are my God!" My future
is in your hands. Rescue me from those
who hunt me down relentlessly.
PSALM 31:13–15 NLT

Many sorrows come to the wicked,
but unfailing love surrounds
those who trust the LORD.
PSALM 32:10 NLT

My enemies would hound me all day,
for there are many who fight against me,
O Most High. Whenever I am afraid,
I will trust in You.
PSALM 56:2–3 NKJV

A non-Davidic psalm summarizes it all when it says, "It is better to take refuge in the LORD than to trust in people" (Psalm 118:8 NLT).

Did you catch that? David says God never fails us and loves us unfailingly. Whenever we are afraid, we can trust Him. What more could we ask of God?

But now, this is what the LORD says—
he who created you, Jacob,
he who formed you, Israel:
"Do not fear, for I have redeemed you;
I have summoned you by name; you are mine.
When you pass through the waters,
I will be with you; and when you pass through
the rivers, they will not sweep over you.
When you walk through the fire,
you will not be burned;
the flames will not set you ablaze.
For I am the LORD your God,
the Holy One of Israel, your Savior.
ISAIAH 43:1–3 NIV

If we truly believe in God, we have nothing to fear. Who is greater than He? Who loves us more than He does?

Trust in God, every moment of every day, even when it's tough. He will never desert you or fail you.

So what are you afraid of? You have nothing to fear.

How can we use tribulations as opportunities to shine for our Lord?

How should we, as Christians, respond to fear?

How can we help others deal with their fear?